A STEP-BY-STEP BOOK ABOUT
DISCUS

GUNTER KELLER

Photography:
Aqua Life Magazine, Japan; Harold Beck; Heiko Bleher; Frickhinger; Dr. R. Geisler; Osvaldo Gonzalez; Charles O. Masters; Hans Mayland; H. Petersmann; Dr. H. H. Reichenbach-Klinke; H. J. Richter; Fred Rosenzweig; Yohei Sakamo; Chuck Sanders; Edward C. Taylor; courtesy Dr. D. Terver, Nancy Aquarium, France.
Drawings by Andrew Prendimano

Distributed in the UNITED STATES by T.F.H. Publications, Inc., One T.F.H. Plaza, Neptune City, NJ 07753; in CANADA to the Pet Trade by H & L Pet Supplies Inc., 27 Kingston Crescent, Kitchener, Ontario N2B 2T6; Rolf C. Hagen Ltd., 3225 Sartelon Street, Montreal 382 Quebec; in CANADA to the Book Trade by Macmillan of Canada (A Division of Canada Publishing Corporation), 164 Commander Boulevard, Agincourt, Ontario M1S 3C7; in ENGLAND by T.F.H. Publications Limited, Cliveden House/Priors Way/-Bray, Maidenhead, Berkshire SL6 2HP, England; in AUSTRALIA AND THE SOUTH PACIFIC by T.F.H. (Australia) Pty. Ltd., Box 149, Brookvale 2100 N.S.W., Australia; in NEW ZEALAND by Ross Haines & Son, Ltd., 18 Monmouth Street, Grey Lynn, Auckland 2, New Zealand; in SINGAPORE AND MALAYSIA by MPH Distributors (S) Pte., Ltd., 601 Sims Drive, #03/07/21, Singapore 1438; in the PHILIPPINES by Bio-Research, 5 Lippay Street, San Lorenzo Village, Makati Rizal; in SOUTH AFRICA by Multipet Pty. Ltd., 30 Turners Avenue, Durban 4001. Published by T.F.H. Publications, Inc. Manufactured in the United States of America by T.F.H. Publications, Inc.

CONTENTS

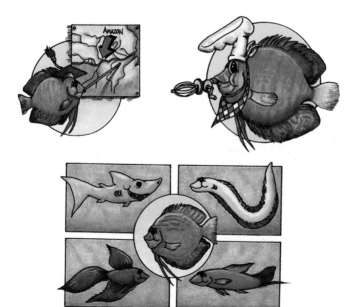

WHAT ARE DISCUS?

Discus have fascinated aquarists and ichthyologists from the time of their introduction into the tropical fish hobby and are the pride of many freshwater aquarists today. They have also posed many problems to their keepers; luckily, solutions to most of those problems have now been found. In addition, discus-keeping has led to new developments in the hobby, and those developments affect the tropical fish field in general in a good way—even people who don't keep discus have benefited from them.

Discus owe their name to their shape, resembling as it does a throwing discus in a vertical position. In the zoological system the discus belongs to the family Cichlidae. The family encompasses many species in many genera, among them the genus *Symphysodon*, which contains nothing but the species of discus. So far, so good—but now come the uncertainties. There is a lot of confusion about the number of species of discus. Some say there is only one species, and some say there are at least two. The ones who say there is only one species base their conclusion on the fact that discus of all types, regardless of color and other superficial differences, interbreed and produce offspring that are 100% fertile themselves. Additionally, they all live in the wild in the same place. The ones who say that there are at least two species base their belief on the fact that ichthyologists have described at least two different species, and separating the two species are (according to the ichthyologists) differences other than color alone.

The systematic division that at present is upheld subdivides the genus *Symphysodon* into two species:

1. *Symphysodon discus* Heckel (true or Heckel discus)

FACING PAGE: This strain of aquarium-bred discus called "royal turkis" was developed by Dr. Eduard Scmidt-Focke, a well-known German discus breeder. Note the absence of vertical body bands usually present in many other discus.

A South American fish collector sorting his catch of the day in the Rio Negro, one of the main tributaries of the Amazon River in Brazil. Lying on his hand is a specimen of *Symphysodon discus.*

2. *Symphysodon aequifasciata* Pellegrin (common or banded discus)

The color varieties of discus are numerous and are known to most discus fanciers by their popular names. These include the brown discus, green discus, blue discus, royal blue discus, turquoise discus, red discus, four-color discus, and pompadour discus, to name just a few. The names for some of these color varieties are mere trade names. The differences in color among them, as compared to the differences in pattern of the species are confusing. Because the two species are so variable and have been hybridized so often, it is impossible to accurately assign the average tank-bred discus to one species or another. When imported wild specimens are available, *S. discus* can usually be told by having the vertical black band in the middle of the body very dark, much more so than the bands before and after it. In *S. aequifasciata* all nine vertical bands are about equally developed. It is probably best to just call most discus *Symphysodon* species and let it go at that.

What are Discus?

The genus *Symphysodon* is confined exclusively to the South American continent, solely to the Amazon and its enormous tributary system. We can, therefore, regard Brazil, Peru, eastern Colombia, and perhaps Venezuela as the home of the discus. Almost 150 years have elapsed since a discus was first described, but the details on where and how the discus live have been discovered only recently.

Close-up photograph of an aquarium-bred discus that can be assigned with confidence to the species *Symphysodon discus*. It has the typical number and characteristics of the body bands of this species.

We know that the discus are not found in the actual stream or main river but in smaller tributaries, backwaters, and smallish lakes. These biotopes are characterized above all by a sometimes very slow current, a low water depth, and relatively steep banks with overhanging and partially immersed branches and roots. The fish seem to have a close attachment to the wood and are almost never seen anywhere but among the roots or among the tree tops or branches that have fallen into the water. The water depth in these places is at least a yard and more. Owing to the color of the water, the dense branches (frequently with leaves), and the floating grass and leaves, they are heavily shaded and relatively dark. Here the discus stand in schools of up to 50 fish. When disturbed, the whole school quickly dives and finds a good hiding place in the dark water among the root thickets.

Catching wild discus is a long, difficult job. The town of Manaus is the point of departure for these expeditions and also the export center for discus in Brazil. A few exporters have settled here, some of them with their own fishing fleets. The fishing areas of the blue and the true discus are roughly a two- to three-day boat journey away from Manaus. The fishing is done by native fishermen, some of whom have moved into houseboats within the fishing area. These fishermen have a good eye for the hiding places of the discus. With long nets that are about 30 feet long and 6 feet broad, these sites (usually tree tops that have fallen into the water) are enclosed in a semi-circle. Then the wood has to be taken out of the enclosure (a slow, difficult task), and the net is dragged along the bottom and ashore. Frequently this entails several hours of labor. Owing to the turbid water, the result can only be seen at the very end. A catch of fifty discus is a good result. Today the fish often are stored and transported in baskets with a plastic lining. This has considerably reduced the danger of injuries as compared to the oil barrels that were used in the past. A total prevention of injuries can, of course, not be achieved, but the minor skin and fin injuries that do occur quickly heal in fresh water.

Discus are also caught at night. When it is dark the fish keep close to the surface, as can also be observed in the aquarium. These places are lit up with the aid of lanterns, and the

This discus is positively a descendant of *Symphysodon aequifasciata* ancestors. The vertical bands are equidistant from each other and are of similar widths.

startled fishes are fished out with large hand nets. When enough have been caught the boat heads back for Manaus. On board, the water the discus are kept in is changed once a day and the containers are covered to protect them against the strong sunshine. At Manaus, the fish are stored in aquaria and plastic containers and shipped out as quickly as possible. According to their size, they are individually packed in plastic bags with oxygen. As a rule, two or three bags are used, as the discus can pierce single bags too easily with their hard fin spines. In addition, the whole thing is often wrapped in several layers of newspaper and then put into yet another plastic bag. Several of these bags are then packed into special Styrofoam boxes. That is how wild discus set out on their long journey by air that eventually leads them into our aquaria—but of course the majority of discus you see in the pet shop are actually imported from the Far East or shipped from Florida, where they are bred in large numbers.

Thanks to modern methods of storage and transport, we now find a good quality stock of discus for sale in pet shops. Some years ago, anyone who kept discus was still a true pioneer; often the animals (wild catches then) could be obtained only if one had special connections and was prepared to spend quite a lot of money. Today a large selection of both wild-caught and commercially raised discus waits for hobbyists who want them. There is no doubt that discus are still comparatively high-priced and, considering how difficult it is to breed them, this is not surprising. But nowadays no aquarist should let himself be deterred from keeping discus as long as he is prepared to abide by a few basic rules, for it is no longer justified to describe discus as problem fish. From our present day knowledge of the structure, behavior, and living requirements of these fish we can adopt many procedures that ensure their successful keeping in the aquarium.

DISCUS IN THE AQUARIUM

THE SETUP

It is obvious that fishes measuring up to 8 inches in diameter and 2¼ inches in body thickness are quite large as aquarium fishes go and require accordingly large containers. How big a discus aquarium ought to be is difficult to say. There is certainly no upper limit, but it should by no means be smaller than 50 gallons. Decisive factors are the number of fishes one intends to keep and how much time one is prepared to dedicate to the care of the water. Apart from the height of the tank (not below 20 inches), one should also take into consideration the

FACING PAGE: Discus are spectacular-looking fishes and they deserve to be displayed in an aquarium that is tastefully decorated. Try to keep a decor that possibly simulates the discus's natural habitat. A variety of South American water plants are available in your local pet shop.

Swordplants (*Echinodorus*) are most appropriate for a discus tank. They are originally from South America, mostly from the Amazon. These plants are both imported and cultivated for the aquarium trade. Shown is a broad-leafed species, *Echinodorus cordifolius.*

size of the tank measured from front to back. It is the front-to-back dimension that provides the discus with room to swim, and it opens up various possibilities for decorating the tank. As a matter of fact, this is where the first conflict arises. For years it was considered necessary, if one wanted to keep discus successfully, to run a "sterile" aquarium. This is a bare aquarium usually equipped with only an up-ended flowerpot or similar object to serve as a hiding or spawning place and probably a few floating plants. This functional setup is designed above all to ensure cleanliness, specifically of the water. Food remnants and feces remain visible and can be removed quickly. For the breeding tank, this can still be recommended today, but in a living room, for instance, an aquarium ought really to form part of the decoration. For this, such a bare and desolate glass box is definitely unsuitable. That is one reason why many aquarists have decided against keeping discus. However, experience has shown that there are other ways and that we need not be deprived of the so-called "esthetic" aquarium after all. By "esthetic" aquarium we mean a tank that can be considered an ornament and is decorated and planted according to the taste of its owner. The esthetic aquarium is perfectly suitable for keeping discus, provided we do not make any fundamental mistakes and take certain factors into consideration.

From the description of the habitat of the discus we can see that in the wild they are found in association with wood. This should be borne in mind, and safe wood should be used wherever possible. Wood in the form of the twisted roots of swamp trees is especially desirable, since it simulates the natural habitat. The bottom of the waters where discus live is mostly sandy, dark, and sometimes thickly covered with leaves. We should take the dark color into consideration. Make sure that the bottom layer we provide does not contain too many soluble minerals or substances that tend to decompose.

The higher plants are absent from those parts of the rivers where discus are caught. This need not deter us, however, from inserting a few rooted plants, such as Amazon sword plants (*Echinodorus*) or others, into the bottom layer. Every plant with a good growth has a beneficial effect on the water. A vital point to remember is to provide shading from above. The fish are used to semi-darkness, and a glaring light over the water surface can make them shy and colorless. A very suitable

A view of a typical area where discus are collected in Tefe, Brazil. Only in rare instances will trees be absent, so they must be cleared out prior to lowering the net or seine. Collecting discus entails some hard labor.

In addition to rooted types of water sprite *(Ceratopteris)*, there are those which float on the water's surface. Such a form can help in shading a discus aquarium from too much light.

floating cover is provided by water sprite (*Ceratopteris*). This plant tolerates soft water, bright light, and high temperatures very well, and its trailing roots make it look interestingly bizarre in the aquarium. A tank with this interior will fascinate every observer, and the fish have a chance to become acclimated quickly and revert to their original habits.

When choosing the bottom layer we have to make sure that we are using the right material and that it does not absorb too much waste matter (feces and uneaten food). The latter can be prevented by careful feeding and a relatively small fish population.

In addition, the water in the aquarium should be filtered. The filter must be readily accessible so that it can be cleaned easily and frequently. What kind of filter one uses is not very important. All kinds and types of filters are being used by discus keepers, and all of them serve their purpose more or less equally well. The function of mechanical filters is to clear the water of turbidity caused by suspended substances. These filters have to be cleaned very often so that the dirt trapped by them does not re-enter the cycle. It is quite astonishing how

quickly such a filter gets filthy. Alternatively, we could let a mechanical filter run as a biological filter. If this is intended, the
filter medium should have a large surface, so we have to use
something similar to coarse quartz gravel. Once the bacteria
have begun to proliferate on the filter medium, the filter is an
excellent aid to nitrification. This kind of filter should not be
cleaned completely at frequent intervals, for cleaning destroys
the active layer of bacteria and the filter becomes ineffective
until new bacteria have accumulated on it. For the additional
chemical treatment of the water one uses activated charcoal
and peat. Activated charcoal is used for the extraction of chemicals, drugs, humic matter, and gases. Peat also is a very useful
material for the treatment of aquarium water. Peat-filtered water has proved excellent where the keeping of discus is concerned. Acid white peat is able, by combining with calcium, to
soften the water and reduce its conductivity. By giving off humic acids, peat is able to lower the pH of water; it also in-
creases its organic substance and gives the water a dark color.
In this way we adapt our water to the natural water in which
the discus live.

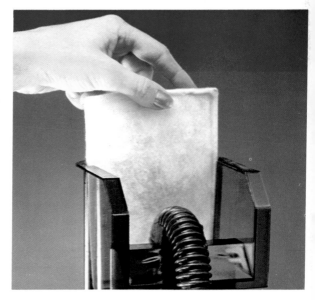

Modern filters are designed for both efficiency and convenience. These disposable cartridges are slightly more costly than loose filter material, but it is worth the bother and time you will save in cleaning your filter.

A discus tank does not require strong aeration. Discus inhabit quiet waters in their natural habitat; they find turbulence disturbing.

For very large tanks, power filters have proved excellent. In tanks with a capacity of below 75 gallons, however, power filters are less good because the discus don't like the strong current they produce. We can observe how tense the fishes stand in the tank, trying to swim against the current. When the pump has been switched off they relax and swim normally, searching the bottom for food. This latter behavior is shown only when conditions in the aquarium are right for them.

WATER

Today it is still widely held that discus can only be healthy—and therefore happy—in water which is absolutely perfect. This is not so. Naturally the fish are not comfortable in any old broth, and we certainly need to give as much attention to the water as it requires, but copying the natural Amazonian waters by using distilled or ionized water is quite unnecessary. The fish tolerate medium-hard or even hard water perfectly well. Very few wholesalers or retailers offer the discus soft wa-

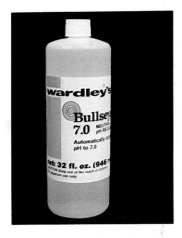

Although water conditioners are available for maintaining a desired pH of aquarium water, it is best to monitor the quality of your water regularly and avoid endangering your fish needlessly. Experienced discus breeders consider water quality an important factor in their success.

ter, yet the fish show no adverse effects. There can be no doubt that it is better for the discus if we add fresh water of medium hardness from time to time rather than try to provide only soft spring water. Lucky is the hobbyist who gets soft water out of the tap, but not many are so lucky. The great majority of aquarists have to adjust the water available to them. Many aquarists are in a position to obtain soft spring water, and such water can be considered ideal. It gets closest to the natural waters of the fish, as long as its conductivity (total salt content) and pH (acidity or alkalinity) are similar too.

A suitable solution has been found in the partial desalting of raw water. Water with a carbonate hardness of two-thirds the total hardness can be easily and efficiently adjusted

In some instances it may be necessary to remove excess chlorine in your aquarium water chemically. Keep a chlorine remover at hand for a possible unforeseen emergency.

with the aid of weak ion-exchangers. By this process the calcium and magnesium ions are exchanged for carbon dioxide. Carbon dioxide quickly grows volatile, and one receives a water that is two-thirds softer. In a larger aquarium the water has to be well aerated, however, before this is done, or the fishes might die of asphyxiation due to an excess of carbon dioxide. Water with, for example, a total hardness of 15 German degrees and a carbonate hardness of 10 degrees has—after the

For added convenience to an aquarist, carbon or charcoal is often incorporated along with the filter material. The mess of disposing of the loose particles of carbon or charcoal that some find unpleasant is eliminated.

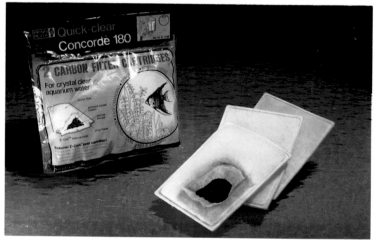

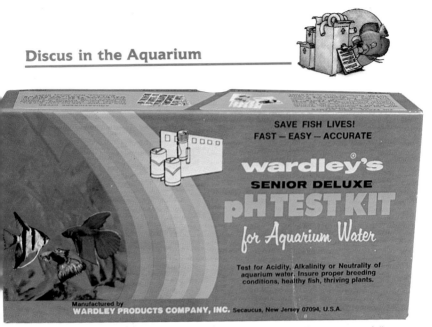

Since the pH of the water is of critical importance in keeping discus successfully, the acquisition of a pH kit is indispensable. All sorts of pH kits are available from the simplest and most basic to the highly technological type used in laboratories.

exchange—a total hardness of no more than 5 German degrees. In water treated in this way and subsequently having a total hardness of 5 German degrees and a carbonate hardness of 1 degree, the wild-caught blue discus in my tank spawned six weeks after I had received them and propagated themselves normally.

Although discus still tolerate pH values down to 4.5, one should not go below a pH of 5; when the water is being changed and the peat filter removed, there is an especially great danger of acidosis. The best method of raising and stabilizing the pH is to add some raw water, provided the latter has a higher carbonate hardness.

It is important that the water not be allowed to become over-loaded with the metabolic waste products of the fish. The waste products, if present in excess, adversely affect the condition of the fish. In particular, growth is retarded, but there can be other negative effects such as general weakening and lower fertility. Here the best method is to use a siphon and a bucket. A partial water change (one quarter of the tank capacity every two weeks) works like magic, and the fish reward us with their liveliness and brilliant colors.

FOOD REQUIREMENTS

More important than anything else when we keep animals is to supply them with a correct diet. It was this aspect above all that seemed to make discus such a problem. Discus had the reputation of being extremely choosy fish that would starve to death rather than take a monotonous diet. Today we know that fish that behave like this are diseased. Healthy discus are not choosy, eat readily, and always have a good appetite. Like most other cichlids, discus are fond of nourishing foods and of insect larvae in particular. We know that mayfly larvae and certain freshwater shrimps are among the food animals taken by wild discus. These particular shrimps are almost impossible to obtain commercially, but that is no reason for us to give up. With the alternative foods available to us, discus can be fed and kept healthy for a long time. When I say "alternative

Those with access to natural ponds may have the opportunity to collect mayfly larvae. Be sure that such a pond is not biologically or chemically polluted, however.

Mosquito larvae can be cultured successfully by a dedicated discus keeper. However, they should not be allowed to develop into adults that can escape back into the wild.

foods," however, I do not mean the dry food that has proved of such value where other fish species are concerned. This is turned down by the discus. Only very young fish have a liking for it, but soon they too demand animal food, and we have to obtain live food for them.

Valuable foods are mosquito larvae and glassworms. When they are in season we should not fail to go around the ponds and collect them. Particularly in the pupal stage, they are a favorite food. In addition, they promote the growth of eggs in many fish species. Bloodworms are another favorite and can be found in large numbers, especially in the winter. But this food can be dangerous. The larvae can be found in the most polluted of waters and may carry a variety of fish-pathogenic organisms or dangerous chemicals. In fact, fish mortalities are not unusual when large quantities of these larvae have been fed to the fish. In addition, the biting apparatus of these larvae can cause injuries inside the stomach of the fish if the larvae have been swallowed whole, and this may cause further mortalities. This risk can be eliminated by feeding frozen bloodworms. All the food animals mentioned so far can be stored in this way. This enables us, particularly during the winter months, to supply our fish with biologically valuable food. That this food has to be defrosted before use goes without saying. If it is not, it can cause inflammations of the stomach and the intestine.

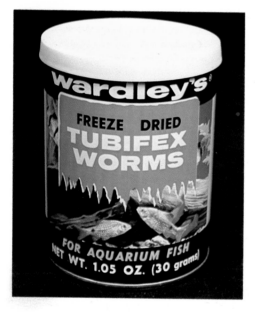

Commercial tubifex worms are usually cleaned rigorously prior to freeze-drying and are relatively safe in comparison to live worms collected from unknown sources. Live worms should always be suspect; this popular food is known to be a positive carrier of fish diseases.

The main food of many discus in our aquaria, and one that is popular with them, is the tubifex worm. But tubifex present much the same problem as bloodworms. Tubifex occur almost exclusively in waste-waters or in brooks with a high content of organic matter. Tubifex also harbor many harmful substances in the intestines and other organs. The worms therefore have to be washed thoroughly. Do not feed tubifex to the virtual exclusion of all else. Such an unbalanced diet upsets the digestion of the fish and results in diarrhea.

Somewhat more advantageous are whiteworms. These home-bred worms are a very nutritious food and should, therefore, be given only in modest amounts. Fatty degeneration of the liver only sets in if enormous quantities of these worms are fed. Three to four whiteworm meals a week—especially when the fish are still growing—can be considered safe and beneficial. Whiteworms as a food have the advantage that they can be washed and enriched with added vitamins.

Discus in the Aquarium

OVERLEAF PHOTO: An array of aquarium-bred discus in a breeder's aquarium. These fancy discus were developed by painstaking selection and breeding of desired strains.

Minced beef heart has proved to be another good substitute for discus natural fare. All fat and fiber are removed from the meat, which is then minced, chopped finely, or—if it is frozen—grated with a kitchen-grater. Once the fish have grown accustomed to this food they develop a liking for it. As far as I know, it has no adverse effects. On the contrary, this food can be conveniently enriched with vitamin preparations available on the market and so becomes an excellent addition to the menu.

Suitable for the fry are water fleas (daphnia), Grindal worms, copepods, and brine shrimp (*Artemia*). The young fish also take freeze-dried foods (whole animals or tablets) and flaked foods. When they can be seen to nibble at soft water plants, feeding with frozen spinach may be indicated. For constant variety in their bill of fare our pets reward us with their quick growth and vitality.

A dish of live daphnia just collected from a natural pond. These tiny crustaceans are easy to collect using a fine-meshed hand net. If aerated, they will survive for a few days in a collecting jar or small aquarium.

HINTS ON KEEPING

Their size limits the number of discus we can keep, and it also makes them undesirable for most community tanks. Their secretive and secluded way of life in their native biotope leads one to assume that they are not fond of too much company. It is true that when wild discus are caught the net frequently contains angelfishes and other cichlids along with them, but discus really look best when kept by themselves. Five or six animals always form an attractive group and bring enough life into any tank. Their color and shape make them such a center of attraction that other fishes become unnecessary. It is important to be aware of the danger of infection the discus would be exposed to if they were constantly subjected to the company of other species. Many ornamental fishes are carriers of parasitic diseases without themselves showing any signs of sickness. Such fishes tolerate their own parasites fairly well but invariably infect discus. Angelfish in particular are a great source of danger in this respect, and constant observation becomes imperative.

There are a large number of color varieties of aquarium-bred discus for any discus lover. Breeders often assign fancy names descriptive of the varieties they produced. The color of many fishes, including discus, can be enhanced by hormones and color enhancers. For example, the red color of fish and other animals can be intensified by a diet rich in carotene.

Discus in the Aquarium

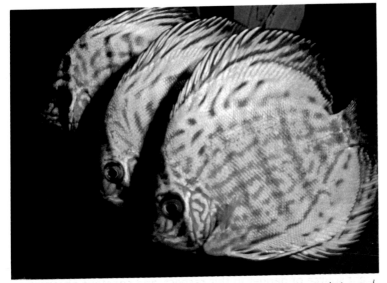

Discus from a single brood are expected to grow at the same rate, but experience shows that at times a single fish can grow much larger than its siblings. Scientists explain this occurrence as being caused by cramped living conditions.

We are lucky that discus are very peaceful cichlids. They do not attack other fishes, except perhaps—but very rarely—small food fishes, and leave the plants where we put them. They can, however, become very shy and nervous if exposed to the wrong environmental conditions. The latter include glaring lights, the sudden appearance of shadows in the aquarium, vibrations, and—above all—a worsening of the water quality. The latter—due to drugs, the wrong pH, or pollution—is easy to remedy. It is, however, possible that this nervous behavior is normal. If the tank provides hiding places similar to those occurring in the natural habitat of the discus, then the fish hurriedly retreat to them whenever they feel threatened. This behavior is particularly common in "adolescent" animals.

If we keep discus under good conditions they will give us much pleasure and we will have the opportunity to study their many modes of behavior and to see our pets grow and reproduce.

BREEDING DISCUS

Healthy and well-nourished discus may be able to reproduce at the age of about 12 months, but to achieve this they have to be fed very well and must be raised under optimal conditions. Aquarists who feed their animals only twice a day are hardly likely to have sexually mature fish within the year. It is therefore not uncommon to observe that under normal conditions one and a half to two years elapse before discus start to reproduce. This delightful and important event announces itself only a few days in advance, but if the animals are closely observed it can be noted in good time. Unfortunately, we are still not able to distinguish the sexes of discus by any external characteristics. In the past there have been many references to structural differences concerning the body, fins, and lips that were interpreted as sex differences (e.g., saddlenose, pointed anal and dorsal fins, separated rays of the ventral fins, and thick lips). From the earliest days of discus-keeping aquarists also believed differences in color to be relevant in the differentiation of the sexes. Today we know that none of the color shades or variations are limited to either sex. It can be observed, however, that the male of a breeding pair is slightly larger and more thick-set as a rule. Where the "royal blue" color variety is concerned, the males often show stronger markings and their overall colors are more intense. But this is not the general rule, and these characteristics have only a limited part to play in the correct determination of the sexes.

With young fish it is definitely impossible to distinguish the sexes with any degree of certainty. One is obliged, therefore, to acquire a number of individuals and leave it to the fish to find each other and get paired off. Before they do so one can observe that a certain hierarchy has established itself in the discus tank. The biggest and most energetic fellow dominates the others absolutely and constantly defends the feeding place. Then come successively subordinate grades, right down to the

The development of discus strains is not the result of indiscriminate breeding, but of a pre-planned procedure that involves basic knowledge of genetics. Pictured here is Schmidt-Focke's royal turkis strain.

last in the pecking order—and that one is pushed around by everyone. Usually this is the smallest fish. Although it always has a good appetite, it is hardly allowed near the food without being dealt a few blows. That such animals show a retarded development is not surprising. Since this pecking order is constantly being put to the test and re-arranged, some hobbyists have been inclined to use it as another aid to sex determination. Fish that were always on the offensive or warded off a head-on collision by lashing out with their tails were thought to be males, while obviously submissive fish were considered to be females. This submissiveness or inferiority was demonstrated by the reduction of the background coloration, increased prominence of the nine crossbands, lowering of the fins, and flight. But this behavior is not confined to a particular sex. It is true that in most cases the fish at the very top of the hierarchy is a male, but there are exceptions even to this rule.

When two fish are ready to mate, their mutual attacks markedly decrease and they often stand together. Courtship begins with the two fish inclining the head slightly as they swim toward each other and literally making a bow. This bow is accompanied by a quick splaying and retracting of the tail fin. At the same time the head usually grows dark in color while the body grows lighter, and the tail fin comes to look sooty black. The male takes the main initiative. Simultaneous with this behavior is a twitching of the dorsal fin. If the female is ready to spawn, she replies with the same signals, and soon after the well-known shaking behavior can be seen. This "shaking" is a horizontal to-and-fro movement carried out with the front part of the body by each partner in turn. At this stage the animals choose a spawning site and then proceed to polish whatever objects happen to be there.

This is usually a moment of conflict for the discus-keeper. Should he take out the potential spawners and transfer them to a breeding aquarium? Or should he leave them in the

FACING PAGE: Confrontations between discus individuals are not unusual. Virile male discus that are ready to breed test each other's strength to determine who will mate with the female. However, these battles seldom lead to great harm to the loser.

It is common practice to remove adult discus intended for breeding from a community display tank. These individuals are juveniles judging from their relative dimensions.

FACING PAGE: A pair of brown and blue discus eyeing closely a possible spawning site—an inverted clay flower pot, the traditional spawning equipment for a discus breeding tank.

Breeding Discus

show tank and take out the other fish? Often one is quite un-
prepared for this situation and another aquarium is not always
available. Then the hobbyist has no choice but to stand back
and see what happens. The removal of the other fish would
cause the least disturbance to the breeders. There have been
instances when broods were raised in the presence of other discus, but this usually results in a certain amount of chaos, and
the risk of failure is high. In a large show tank it invariably becomes a problem to feed the fry, and not many of them are
likely to survive into adulthood.

Submerged broken branches of trees provide spawning substrates for discus in this part of the river in Tefe, Brazil.

One is well-advised, however ~~~~~~ fish spawn in their familiar surroundings for ~~~~~~ing and to watch what is going on. In this way ~~~~un find out: a) whether the "newly-weds" really are male ~~~nd female; b) whether they get along with each other; and c) whether the eggs have been fertilized. There have been many occasions when two animals of

In another discus habitat in Tefe, the broad buttressing roots that extend into the water of massive trees growing along the banks are used as spawning sites.

In this area in Rio Abacaxis, Brazil, flat slabs of stones along the bank are without doubt utilized as spawning substrate by discus known to be present here.

the same sex showed the most convincing mating behavior but, after they had rashly been separated from the other fish, presented the greatest difficulty when the aquarist tried to "breed" them.

In their natural environment, discus presumably deposit their spawn on submerged trees or roots. If available, the same spawning substrate is chosen in the aquarium, but discus also select large stones, large plant leaves, the glass panes of the aquarium, the heater or thermostat, etc. The chosen spawning site is freed from algae, dirt, and slime. The broad-leaved plants suffer most in this respect; often they are seriously damaged by the vigorous cleansing activity of the fish. The chances of good results are slim when the eggs have been deposited on leaves. Over the years, flowerpots or vases made of clay have become firmly established as spawning substrates. This method has proved particularly successful in "sterile"

breeding aquaria. Usually when the spawning pair is fished out of the show tank and transferred to this type of breeding tank, their breeding instinct is interrupted. The fish need some time to get used to their new surroundings, but luckily in most cases the mating urge soon returns. This kind of tank, which need not be too large (35 to 50 gallons), offers the best guarantee for successful breeding. As a rule, the animals spawn in the evening whether the light is on or not.

At this time it becomes possible to determine the sexes by observing the structure of the genital papilla. The female's ovipositor protrudes noticeably more and its breadth appears to remain constant. In the male, on the other hand, the genital papilla narrows down like a cone. At this stage the color of the fish also changes. They may grow so dark as to appear almost black. Only the caudal peduncle sometimes remains light. This coloration is most marked during the actual act of spawning. It must be added, however, that it is not of the same intensity in all discus and all varieties, nor does the color give us any indication as to whether the parents are likely to care for their brood or not.

To lay the eggs, the female approaches the spawning site from below. She retracts her fins and the eggs emerge like a string of pearls. The eggs are slightly yellowish and have a diameter of about 1 mm.

This is where an up-ended flowerpot proves invaluable. Owing to the pot's relatively large surface area, the discus female can spread out each egg-chain and leave a greater space between them. This is an advantage, for if the eggs die and become fungused, the parent animals remove them, but with their large mouths they invariably damage the eggs close by. What they end up destroying sometimes outweighs the intended improvement. If the eggs lie on a narrow branch or leaf or some equally small space, they are very close together and frequently piled on top of each other as well. In this case the

FACING PAGE: A female discus depositing eggs on a broad leaf blade, as the male patiently waits for his turn to fertilize the eggs.

losses caused by the parents when they try to pick out the bad ones are particularly high.

The male fertilizes each egg-chain as soon as it has been laid, always giving the impression of sizing up the eggs with its "nose" before it swims across them and distributes the sperm. It is accompanied by severe "shaking" of both fish. It can also happen, however, that both partners carry out their functions simultaneously. Equally possible, unfortunately, is that the female lays her eggs and the male shows no interest in breeding or is distracted by an observer. We should then get

This breeding discus pair has elected to spawn on a clay cylinder laid upright on one side of the aquarium. Note the much darker coloration of the fish below. Such color changes can be expected during the breeding cycle—from courtship until the end of the brooding period.

away from the tank and leave the fish to themselves. Often we are forced to watch how certain males leave the eggs unfertilized and quickly swallow them.

The number of eggs depends on the condition, nutrition, and size of the parents. Wild catches not infrequently produce 300 to 400 eggs per clutch, but 200 is a good average. When spawning is over each animal by turn fans the eggs with its pectoral fins, thereby supplying them with water that has a high oxygen content while at the same time removing dirt particles and small organisms.

Often the first problem of discus breeding arises at this stage: a wrong reaction by one or both of the parents when engaged in caring for the brood. Very often one can at this point observe eating of the eggs, a discus vice. One partner shows itself unwilling to look after the brood, pushes the "nursing" animal away from it, and proceeds to swallow the eggs. This behavior is not confined to the discus but can be observed in other cichlids as well. The angelfish is perhaps the greatest expert in this respect, which explains why it is almost always reared artificially. How the eating of the eggs can be prevented

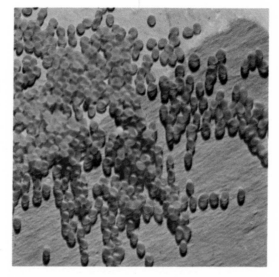

Appearance of a healthy clutch of eggs laid on a large piece of rock in a public aquarium. Only one egg at the center is obviously opaque; it is already dead, possibly unfertilized.

we do not know. Many experiments have been carried out using different methods, but none proved successful. In many cases we are lucky and things simply sort themselves out. After having eaten its previous clutches, a pair may suddenly look after its latest brood with the utmost care. Young fish show a marked tendency to indulge in egg-eating. The aquarist must keep his nerve and exercise great patience. Should the abnormal behavior persist over a long period, then the fish are unsuitable for breeding to each other and must be exchanged. Often there is instant success with the new partner.

THE FRY

The key to success in breeding discus is to have a pair of fish that take good care of the brood. This need not necessarily be the pair that originally found one another. Often the dominant males are the first to get a female to spawn, but then they show their true nature and eat or abandon the eggs. It is preferable, therefore, to always keep a number of discus so that changes can be made. It should not be necessary to point out how important it is to feed the animals well when they get ready to spawn. Particularly suitable at this time are insect larvae. An occasional dose of vitamin-enriched food can be recommended, too. To some extent this will also help to reduce the parents' appetite for their eggs.

Let us return to the normal, however. Here we see one fish, often both, engaged in fanning the eggs. The head is light-colored now, almost yellowish, and the body is dark. This characteristic "nursing color" is not always fully displayed, however. Perhaps this is due to the aquarium and its own surroundings.

Kept at a temperature of 82–86°F, the brood hatches within 50–60 hours. Often they are assisted by their parents, who suck them out of the egg cases and then attach them to another part of the spawning substrate. At this stage the larvae are not yet able to swim and derive the necessary nourishment from their yolk sac. The larva has three pairs of glands on the head that secrete a mucous substance by means of which the larva becomes attached to objects. This secretion is vital; without it, the larva would sink to the bottom of the dark waters in its natural habitat and inevitably perish. But because of it, the parent animals can deposit their brood on a suitable surface and constantly keep an eye on them. Larvae that wriggle themselves free and sink to the bottom are caught in the mouth and spat back into their place. Again the flowerpot, with its sloping sides and the rim where the larvae become attached, proves highly suitable.

This male turquoise discus is fanning the eggs with his pectoral fins. A steady current of highly oxygenated water is critical during the incubation period. This chore is shared by both parents, alternately or together.

Installing an ultraviolet sterilizer can reduce the bacterial growth in the water. Select the type designed to fit your setup for maximum efficiency.

I should mention here that at this stage the aquarium must be scrupulously clean and that above all the water must be in good condition, i.e., low in bacteria and not saturated with waste matter. This is best achieved with peat filtration. Another good aid is a UV sterilizer, particularly where we wish to combat water turbidities caused by bacteria. Nursing pairs are now very busy with their young and will transfer them to another locality from time to time. At this time we have to choose the parents' food with extra care. Generally speaking,

Frozen adult brine shrimp is intended for the parents, the baby or newly hatched brine shrimp for the fry.

Nobody can predict whether a discus parent will devour the eggs or the hatched fry at a later time. Taking the responsible parent out of the tank is the best course of action.

anything that wriggles should be avoided, for in most cases this kind of food is misidentified by the parents and spat into the same place as the wriggling brood. Whole bunches of larvae which then become attached to, say, a tubifex worm can sink as a result and be lost. To avoid this risk, it is best to give frozen food to the parents. This food does not move and is swallowed without hesitation.

The larval stage lasts three to four days, then the brood begins to grow independent. We have now come to another decisive phase. The wriggling movements of the larvae have gained in intensity over the last few hours, and the first larvae now succeed in detaching themselves from the spawning substrate and swim off immediately. The first of the escapees are recaptured by the parents and spat back into their place, but usually they set off again right away, and the number of larvae swimming toward their parents is constantly growing. The parents give up their hopeless attempts to keep the brood together and—very dark in color now—quietly stand in front of the brood.

Discus emit a skin secretion that serves as nourishment for the young for the first few days after they have become able to swim actively. Often this secretion can be seen before the larvae swim free, as it forms a milky gray deposit on the backs of the parent animals.

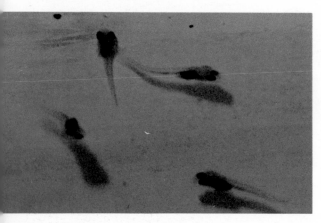

Some breeders, like the noted American discus breeder Jack Wattley, raise the brood completely apart from the parents by feeding them a special formula. Shown are two of such fry.

This skin secretion is vital for the young, as they do not ingest any other food for at least the first two to four days. How the young find their way to the source of nourishment is still not known. Normally, the brood swims toward the parents by the shortest possible route and proceeds to "graze" on the secretion, usually starting on the head and the back and then working onto the dorsal fin. Scent and visual signals are thought to be responsible for the tracking down of the food source, but there have been occasions when whole broods could be observed to swim past the parents although the skin secretion was clearly visible. If the young fail to find the way to the parents within the shortest possible time, they invariably perish. They stray around the aquarium for a few more hours

Judging from the size of the head and shape of the body, these discus fry are very young and just starting to feed on the secretion of the parents' skin.

These discus fry are possibly large enough to accept small foods (flakes, frozen or freeze-dried).

and then disappear. Usually the parents try very hard to keep the brood at the food source. Escapees are carefully pursued and caught with the mouth. The young fish is "chewed" briefly and spat out again. As a rule it then swims toward the parent without delay and joins its siblings that are busily feeding.

For the first few hours both parents offer themselves to the brood as "grazing grounds." Later, however, one parent detaches itself from the brood by suddenly swimming off very quickly, and the young all change over to the other parent. After a short time—seconds to minutes later—the first parent swims to the partner with the young and, by twitching its fins, lures the brood toward it. The released fish, in turn, swims off now and takes a break. Since the great majority of the brood start to swim in the morning, they have practically all day to stuff themselves with food.

Toward the evening many discus pairs gather their young together again by picking them up and spitting them back into the spawning place. Here the young reattach themselves to the mucous threads still present and spend the night just as they did during the larval stage. This behavior can not be observed in all animals, however. Often the parents can be seen to leave the brood on their bodies, making no attempt to collect the young. Where this is the case we should leave a weak light on during the night. If one suddenly turns off the

Feeding the fry is shared by both parents. In this photo, the swarm is in the process of moving from one parent to the other.

light, it will not be long before the young start to wander through the tank, and by morning there may already be fewer of them, or the ties with their parents will have been severed, causing the fry to flee. It thus is advisable to leave on a weak lamp over the spawning place for the first two nights after the young have become able to swim.

When the brood is grazing on the body of a parent, evidence of food intake can be seen a few hours later. By this time the bellies of the young have grown bigger and are visibly filled with a white mass. At this stage one can say that the major ob-

A young discus, beside being small, has a longer body in relation to the depth or height of the body.

stacle in discus breeding has been overcome, but there may be a few more difficulties yet, for the eggs are not the only thing the parent discus can show themselves partial to. A similar phenomenon can also be found during the larval stage of the young. At the end of a quarrel in front of the brood it often happens that the whole brood is swallowed. Such discus tend to indulge themselves again if they get the chance and have to be watched very carefully. If they repeat this behavior several times, we have to exclude them from breeding. Fortunately they are in the minority. More common, on the other hand, is

This juvenile discus already shows a normal disc-shaped body, an adult charac-ter. This is achieved by different growth rates of body length and height.

a quarrel over who carries the young. The partner who is carry-ing them feels reluctant to change over again and would like to keep them. Then we can witness scenes of "jealousy" that are accompanied by attacks and biting. This is not good for the young fish; they now cling so tightly to the parent they happen to be with that they are prevented from feeding. Often each parent has some of the young and tries to lure the rest away from its mate. The strong twitching of fins puts the fry into a state of alarm, and they nestle up to the parent and keep per-fectly still.

A dark variety of discus surrounded by a swarm of fry. A few of them are directly feeding on the surface of the parent's body.

These occasional rows can be regarded as normal quarrels, and we should not interfere. But if an individual fish makes trouble all the time, constantly attacking its partner and even taking out its bad temper on the young by snapping at them, it is often better to separate the pair. The parent the young are with most of the time should be left in the tank and the other fished out. Although breeding success becomes doubtful, the risk of failure was much greater while the two parents were fighting. Fish that previously showed themselves reluctant to hand over the young to their mate often continue to look after the brood on their own. Usually their supply of skin secretion is adequate, too.

The brood must have been feeding on the skin secretion for at least two days before we can hope to keep them alive on some sort of substitute food, but even then the result is far from good, and if the young survive they grow very slowly. For this reason, attempts have been made to raise discus fry artificially. The "nutrient slime" of discus was carefully analyzed. It was thought that the secretion perhaps also served as a culture medium for protozoans, which formed the primary nourishment of the grazing discus fry. Apparently this is not so, because the examined slime was free from unicellular organisms.

Many attempts have been made to raise and feed discus artificially, but few are simple enough or reliable enough for the beginner. They usually involve powdered egg mixtures fed in special ways to an exacting schedule.

How important the skin secretion is can be seen from the fact that in the early stage the young almost double their body length from day to day. If the parents look after their brood peacefully, the fry have constant access to this nourishment and can be seen to graze without interruption. Sometimes the "slime" seems to be a bit on the tough side, and one can observe that the young really have to tug at it and twist it around before they manage to tear off their mouthful.

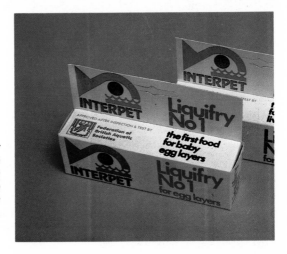

Those unable or unwilling to prepare special fry food can elect to purchase commercially prepared fry food.

Flake food (brine shrimp, tubifex, and others) can be reduced to smaller pieces to fit smaller mouths.

Four to six days may elapse before it becomes necessary for us to offer any supplementary food to the fry. Dependence on the skin secretion (and thus on the parents) is so strong at first that the young do not go after free-swimming food. We cannot do better than to start off with live baby brine shrimp, an ideal supplementary food. The young discus chase after these nauplii even after they are well past the fry stage. When we feed the fry with *Artemia*, it is an advantage to use a smallish breeding tank with a smooth bottom. In this way the fish can find all the nauplii they have been given, including those that are already half-dead and lying on the bottom. In a large, decorated tank this would not be so easy.

Another suitable food that ensures good growth is Grindal worms. These small cultured worms can be mashed and enriched with added vitamins.

When we start to feed the young on regular foods, we need to change the water at frequent intervals. This also promotes good growth. A powerful filter should not be connected to the aquarium during the first few days of independent swimming. Many a discus brood has been known to vanish inside of one.

Once the fry have started to accept a supplementary food we no longer need to be so particular about keeping the water hardness very low. Of course we should continue to check the pH and make sure that it does not rise above 7. Owing to the large supplies of food in a small space, the decomposition of proteins could well result in the formation of ammonia.

Although the young fish are now at the stage where they derive most of their nourishment from live food, they still continue to swim to the parents for more of the skin secretion. Sometimes they actually go so far as to injure the skin and eat holes into it. The skin tissue seems to taste particularly good. Now it is high time to separate the young from their parents. Generally speaking, one should leave the fry with their parents for three to four weeks. By this age they take almost anything they can swallow. They eat copepods, small water fleas, finely chopped tubifex and beef heart as well. This is also the time when we can introduce them to dry food. Experiments with mixed foods containing agar have also proved very successful. These foods were made up of calf's liver and spleen, water fleas, mosquito larvae, and a variety of commercial dry foods, turned into a mash in the mixer and bound with agar-agar.

Young discus are temperamental and forever hungry. Even when they are no bigger than the size of a thumbnail, they fight over bits of food. They should, therefore, be fed several times a day. In this way they grow better, and they also have a greater resistance to diseases. They definitely should have variety in their diet.

Live brine shrimp, both adult and newly hatched, are sold in pet shops. You can hatch them, too, at home in a simple brine shrimp egg hatching setup.

DISEASES

The diseases to which they are subject are one big reason why discus have always been considered to be a problem fish. It took some years for the problems to be identified and, with the aid of science, gradually cleared up. Many aquarists have been forced to look on helplessly as the discus in their aquaria grew apathetic, refused all food, and then slowly but surely died. All the tricks that could be thought of were tried, but in the end it had to be admitted that the fish were suffering from diseases for which there was no known cure.

Discus can contract a great variety of diseases. Since a fish, like other animals, is able to cope with a certain number of parasites, it may be diseased without this becoming apparent to us. The first signs of ill health are reflected in color changes and behavior changes. Good observation is, therefore, always essential. Unfortunately we seldom get hold of discus that are free of parasites. Wild-caught discus in particular are often infested with tapeworm larvae and other parasites. The emphasis in caring for the discus, therefore, must be placed on the providing of natural conditions so that we help to build up the resistance of the fish.

The following are a few of the more common problems seen in discus. Several can be cured with drugs available in the pet shop, but others, including several not discussed, cannot be successfully treated.

ACIDOSIS

Water that is too acid can cause severe damage to the fish. Where we have very soft water in combination with peat

FACING PAGE: This beautiful variety of fancy discus is named the "checkerboard" discus on account of the almost regular reticulated color pattern. It is in the best of health—intact and well-formed fins, brilliant coloration, clear and bright eyes, and so on.

filtration, the risk of acidosis is highest. Affected fish grow dark in color and seem reluctant to swim. Often, however, they may shoot through the tank as if panic–stricken. After prolonged exposure to excessively acid water the skin shows patches of milky turbidity and the formation of thickened white areas can be seen. One should not allow the pH to drop below 5. Treat the condition by raising the pH by changing the water, using a new water having a higher alkalinity and carbonate hardness. Commercial products designed to alter the pH are also available.

SKIN TURBIDITY

Where skin and fins of the discus show a gray deposit—usually clearly visible owing to the dark coloration of the

Trichodina is a parasitic ciliate affecting the skin and gills of freshwater fishes. If present in large numbers it can kill fish.

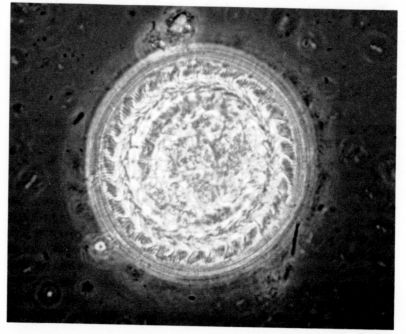

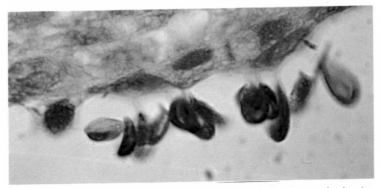

Costia is a common flagellated parasite of the skin and gills of many freshwater fishes. A healthy fish maintained in good water conditions rarely suffers any harm from the presence of this parasite.

fish at such times—they are likely to be infested with protozoans. The latter may be skin parasites of the genera *Costia*, *Chilodonella*, or *Trichodina*, or belong to an *Oodinium* species. These parasites also attack the gills and cause the fish to breathe faster. Infected fish usually retract the fins and scrape

Oodinium cysts in the gill tissues can drastically weaken a fish by reducing the respiratory capacity of the gills to absorb oxygen.

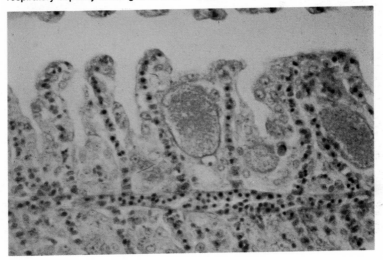

themselves on firm objects. A precise diagnosis is possible only with the aid of skin smears under the microscope.

Since a great variety of causative agents can be controlled with the same drugs, commercial treatments are generally applicable in such cases. Discuss the problem with the people of your pet shop.

SPIRONUCLEUS

Spironucleus is a protozoan that gives much trouble to the discus. This parasite, also known under the name *Hexamita*, is a flagellate that lives in the intestine of discus but can also invade other organs, which are destroyed by it. This flagellate is responsible for the early death of many discus. The worst aspect of an infection with these flagellates is that in the early

Hexamita can reproduce in large numbers and result in an epidemic in a fish tank.

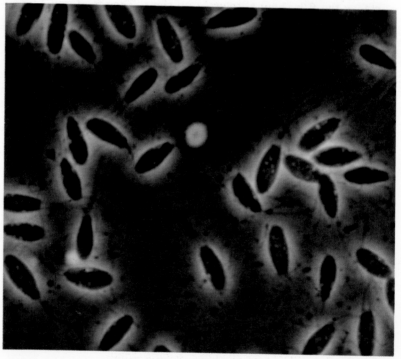

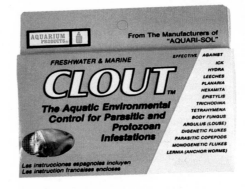

Application of a general anti-parasitic medication may be effective in the control of common freshwater fish parasites (protozoan and metazoan). However, be sure to follow closely the instructions for its use.

stages the fish show absolutely no signs. They feed and swim normally, and their behavior and coloration remain unchanged. Then they suddenly grow fussy about what they eat, and soon they refuse to eat altogether. Their feces look thin, slimy, and white, and the animals grow increasingly apathetic. By the time these obvious signs have appeared the disease has reached a very advanced stage and it is almost too late.

Experience has shown that it is virtually impossible to obtain discus that do not harbor these parasites. In addition, the constant danger of infection with flagellates excreted in the feces is particularly great in the aquarium. Good, though temporary, success has been achieved by raising of the temperature to 98°F for two to three days. Good aeration is essential. Many a fish has been saved in this way and was freed of other parasites at the same time, but the possibility of a relapse must never be excluded.

Better results are achieved by means of chemotherapy, using commercial remedies specifically formulated to combat *Spironucleus*. Enheptin, Cyzine, carbarsone oxide, and dimetridazole have been used with varying degrees of success. Healthy fish suffer no adverse effects if they are chemically treated every three to six months. Caution is advisable: relapses have occurred, presumably because of resistant strains.

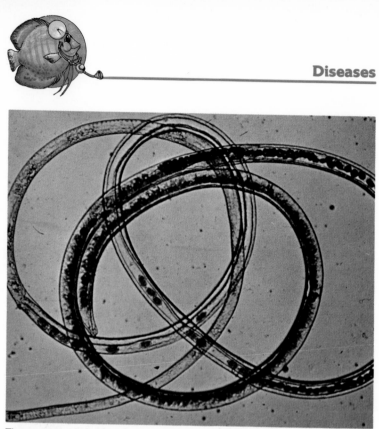

The round bodies inside the body cavity of this specimen of *Capillaria*, a parasitic nematode of fish, are developing eggs. They leave the body of the fish along with the feces.

THREADWORMS

Threadworms of the genus *Capillaria* pose a big threat to the life of our discus. These worms are very thin, one-half to one inch long, and live in the intestine of the fish. The only way to find out whether threadworms are present is to examine the feces. The worms lay many eggs, and these eggs are constantly discharged with the feces. The small oval structures look as though they had been sealed with champagne corks at either end.

Frequently, the behavior of the fish indicates that they are infested with worms. If the discus stand perfectly still in the aquarium, barely swimming and eating, with a conspicuous

tendency to stand facing the back wall, and their bellies look slightly distended, they are almost certainly suffering from *Capillaria* infestation. The feces may be thin and white, as the worms fix themselves to the intestinal wall and destroy it.

Your pet shop has medications to control threadworms, but the course of treatment may be long, complex, and not certain of success.

HOLE-IN-THE-HEAD DISEASE
Although the majority of discus keepers have made the acquaintance of this disease, scientists are still not able to tell us its exact causes. The main characteristic of this disease

Typical appearance of a lesion of hole-in-the head.

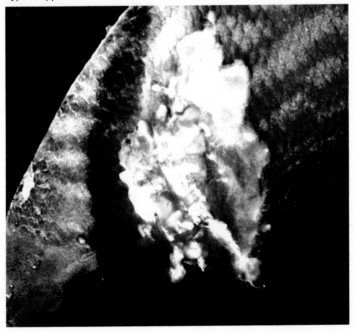

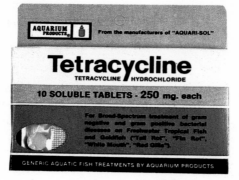

Certain antibiotics, like Tetracycline, are effective in the control of bacterial diseases of fish. Antibiotics are sold in various forms; as a liquid, in powder form, in tablets, or pills.

is the growth of a small stringy white substance in the skin, usually in the head region, particularly on the forehead and above the eyes. This phenomenon might almost be said to resemble a prominent mole. This growth goes away and leaves a relatively large hole behind. If the water is very clean—i.e., containing few bacteria—and the fish look healthy and strong, the hole quickly closes up again and soon ceases to be visible. But if we are less lucky, the hole grows septic and may develop into a large festering sore. Such animals are in acute danger and must be treated.

Treatment is aimed mainly at the infection. Very effective in this respect is Rivanol, and good results are also achieved with antibiotics such as Terramycin or sulfanilamide. Follow manufacturer's instructions.

Fish suffering from hole-in-the-head disease usually continue to have good appetites. At the first signs of the disease it is advisable to change the diet and provide food that is particularly rich in vitamins. This can be done by enriching normal food with commercial aquarium vitamin preparations. At the same time we should ensure that the water in the tank is fresh and biologically perfect. In this way we can usually stop the disease and for years continue to keep discus without a recurrence.

The following books by T.F.H. Publications are available at pet shops everywhere.

Suggested Reading

CICHLIDS OF THE WORLD—By Dr. Robert J. Goldstein
ISBN 0-87666-032-4
T.F.H. H-945
A comprehensive book on the most popular group of fishes, the family that includes the sought-after discus fishes. For the avid aquarist who specializes or wants to specialize in cichlids. A must for the reference library of advanced aquarists, dealers, fish importers. Written for the high school level.
Hard cover, 5½ x 8", 382 pages; 104 black and white photos, 270 color photos.

ALL ABOUT CICHLIDS—By Braz Walker
ISBN 0-876622-038-0; TFH PS-751
This very practical and useful book makes a splendid first acquisition for any aquarist who'd like to learn more about a fascinating fish family without getting too heavily involved in the systematics of the group. It goes light on the taxonomical approach and concerns itself almost entirely with purely practical considerations: how to feed cichlids, how to house them, how to breed them, how to raise the fry, how to recognize and treat diseases, etc.
Hard cover, 5½ x 8", 96 pages; contains many color photos in addition to black and white.

HANDBOOK OF DISCUS—By Jack Wattley
ISBN 0-86622-037-2; TFH H-1070
One of the foremost discus authorities and breeders in the world (he developed the famous Wattley Turquoise) has now written the most comprehensive work on the subject ever published for scientists, hobbyists, fish culturists and students. The text includes detailed information on spawning, discus farming, and disease recognition and treatment.
Hard cover, 8½ x 11", 112 pages. Over 100 full-color photos.

Index